HILL COUNTRY WINE CAVE

CLAYTON
KORTE

HILL COUNTRY WINE CAVE

Architecture by Clayton Korte

Foreword by Tom Kundig FAIA RIBA
Introduction by Jordan Mackay
Principal Photography by Casey Dunn
Additional Photography by
Korta Photography and Brodie Kerst
On Inevitability and Character by Canan Yetmen
Edited by Oscar Riera Ojeda

OSCAR RIERA OJEDA
PUBLISHERS

Table of Contents

Foreword

by Tom Kundig FAIA RIBA

There's no question that Texas Hill Country is an untamed place. You get a sense of this wildness in the open sky and jagged limestone cliffs of the Edwards Plateau. This rugged landscape demands an architectural response that is both lawless and functional, practical yet transformational. Clayton Korte instinctively understands this essence, applying a contemporary lens to the centuries-old practice of storing wine in caves, creating architecture that is sensitive to the land rather than imposing upon it.

Humans have always been fascinated by caves. They were our earliest forms of shelter and symbolized gateways of transformation in myths and legends. Excavating and building within a limestone cave continues that narrative of practicality transformed. It's a bold yet restrained choice that feels familiar and enigmatic all at once. Clayton Korte has crafted architecture in Texas Hill Country for years, and their ability to tread lightly on the land is reflected in the Hill Country Wine Cave. Their design uses technical precision to navigate the challenges of working within a subterranean cave while allowing the "non-building" to emerge as an organic extension of the hillside, as if it has always belonged to this landscape.

From arrival, Clayton Korte plays with the tension between opacity and transparency, using solids and voids to alternately hide and expose the cave's form. The raw limestone exterior gives way to a refined "wooden box" interior that humanizes the mysterious void. It strikes a balance between prospect and refuge: the glass-walled entrance draws in natural light and frames views of the cypress trees, while the cave is unexpectedly warm and intimate.

Hill Country Wine Cave challenges the traditional focus of architecture, which draws our gaze outwards and upwards. Instead, Clayton Korte pulls our attention inward, grounding us within the earth itself. This subterranean setting turns the simple act of storing and enjoying wine into an immersive experience rooted in the history, culture, and untamed nature of Texas Hill Country.

Introduction

by Jordan Mackay

"Until I was nearly forty," wrote George Saintsbury in his 1920 classic of wine literature, *Notes on a Cellar-Book,* "such liquids as I possessed had to endure very inferior accommodation." One wine cellar, he recalled, "... at certain times of the year used to be filled about a foot deep with the most pellucid water, apparently rising from the earth ... [which] necessitated the erection of a plank bridge to get to the wine and incidentally made the house above rather damp." Saintsbury clearly lacked the services of a good architect.

More than a century later, Brian Korte and Cam Greenlee of the architecture and design firm Clayton Korte, would find themselves clad in knee-high rubber boots, standing in nearly 18 inches of water in a 75-foot-long excavated hillside tunnel beneath the celebrated Hill Country of Central Texas. Their job was to figure out how to turn this damp but expansive cave into a functional wine cellar. The excavation had been done by a contractor but no one had put much thought into how to build a wine cave or what it should look like, hence the call to the Clayton Korte team, known by the contractor to have worked on wine-related projects in the past. That the ultimate structure would become arguably one of the most mesmerizing and admired constructions in the (unchronicled and generally tedious) history of wine storage would have been at this moment impossible to imagine.

Wine cellars needn't be pretty. The task of wine storage has only four simple conditions. The storeroom must be secure, dark, and stable in its cool temperature and (moderate) humidity. Putting it out of sight, deep underground is a most sensible option. Indeed, the great tradition of subterranean storage happens to exist across many of the world's greatest wine regions. In the Loire Valley, for instance, the sprawling caves known as troglodyte cellars date back to at least the Gallo-Roman era and, in addition to wine, have for centuries housed families, farm animals, and even restaurants and hotels. In Burgundy, no greater pleasure exists than to be invited down into a vigneron's mold-covered limestone basement to sample from barrel his luminous Chardonnays and Pinot Noirs. In Champagne, astonishingly vast tunnels stretch for miles underneath villages holding millions of slowly maturing bottles.

American wine caves are different. They tend not to occur naturally and must be dug at great cost, generally by deep-pocketed wineries that can afford such things. Because they are such sizable financial and logistical undertakings, caves dug by the wine industry tend to be larger than needed for barrel and bottle storage and end up being put to other purposes, such as dining, entertaining, and drinking. From his experience designing for winery clients in California's Central Coast, Brian Korte knew this about American wine caves, and, standing in that flooded cave, his mind began to churn.

The Hill Country setting for this project differed from the firm's other wine-related jobs—the landscape wasn't coastal California and the client wasn't a commercial winery with barrels and bottling lines but simply an oenophile with a large ranch and bottles to store.

This excavated cave doesn't lie in close proximity to the client's ranch house. Rather, visitors approach it by car or foot, crossing a bridge over a lazy river. In this short journey, the visitor passes through a breathtaking natural setting: a tangled wilderness that nevertheless boasts a grace and gentleness that explains why humans have inhabited this area continuously for 12,000 years. Just out of sight of the cave entrance, the river twists around a bend, traveling through a narrow valley bordered by towering chalk cliffs, tree-studded hillsides, and grasslands dotted with gnarled oak and cedar. The overall effect is meditative, a Texan take on Chinese landscape painting, which expresses life's duality by juxtaposing static, timeless mountains with the mutability of flowing water.

In their projects set in a landscape, Clayton Korte's style is first and foremost to highlight the site's native beauty. "Buildings can partner with a beautiful setting, remaining subservient and quiet, while carrying their own beauty as

stewards of the place," Korte has remarked. He uses terms like "non-building" to describe this work, noting that "we go out to a site for the first time, and it's so pretty that our initial thought is 'we cannot screw this up.'"

The wine cave project offered a unique opportunity to spin this notion to an extreme. Viewed from the outside, the cave's mouth is nothing but a minor interruption in a glorious landscape. Yet the cave mouth doesn't go unnoticed. Its presence—and the mystery it automatically proposes—claws at us, providing an inescapable injection of drama into an otherwise pastoral scene.

Caves possess an almost supernatural power over us. After all, they were the cradles of humanity—early humans' first shelters beyond their mothers' wombs. It was on the walls of caves that they etched their first artistic expressions. But as much as caves represent safety and warmth, they are also foreboding—dark places into which one can disappear and be lost forever, swallowed up by the earth itself.

Thus, caves are primal symbols in human psychology. They represent inner consciousness, the dream world, the void. To Freud, they "[enclose] a space capable of being filled by something" and thus signify female sexuality and fear of the unknown. For Jung, caves can be salutary, "a place of meditation and of the mystery of transformation from the earthly to the heavenly, from the carnal to the spiritual."

If this cascade of associations seems overwrought, consider the arresting visual power of Clayton Korte's Hill Country Wine Cave. Standing outside—even regarding the photos in this book—you can't peel your eyes from it. This is deliberate. This is good design that reaches deep into our brains' limbic systems and doesn't let go.

The entrance to the cave cannot be seen from the river or much of the surrounding landscape. Indeed, it seems to be trying to hide from view, concealed by the hillside itself, which only strengthens one's desire to enter it. This is Clayton Korte's intent, as the entrance is sunk a few feet below ground level and partially obscured by massive limestone boulders collected during the excavation. Above it grows a riot of vegetation, with tangled trees climbing the hillside and ivies and vines scaling the outer surfaces. In daylight the floor-to-ceiling windows of the portal reflect the surrounding rock and vegetation, providing a striking sheen of mirrored modernity. An embedded limestone terrace flows into uneven, uncut stone steps that angle down to a small grotto court surrounding the windows and tall, solid-wood door. The juxtaposition is jarring—like stepping into the future via Stonehenge.

Dug 18 feet into solid limestone, the cave's north-facing entrance needed shoring up to protect the glass and doorway from scree tumbling off the fracturing hillside and damaging vegetal growth. To that end, a thick bulkhead protrudes over and around the front façade, A barricade of sorts—Korte and Greenlee have described it as a "silent sentinel" —it provides a bunker-like impermeability, designed to weather harsh conditions for eons. Made from board-formed concrete and acting as a thermal break, the bulkhead itself becomes an essential visual component. Its horizontally lined relief pattern echoes not only the sedimentary limestone strata of the cliffs facing the cave but also the wood paneling of the interior, accenting the sense of transition and transformation.

Entering the wine cave, we experience a journey from unspoiled nature to the cordial embrace of human design, highlighted by the material transitions from raw limestone exterior to the shotcrete and sculpted stone-plaster cave walls to the linear patterns of board-formed concrete into the warm embrace of wood-paneling and organic materials.

When Clayton Korte first saw it, the cave's post-excavation raw stone walls had already been reinforced with rebar and shotcrete. A decorative layer of cement plaster had been applied and sculpted to look like natural stone. In his initial proposal of a combination of wine storage and a cozy lounge, Korte's inclination was to simply plaster over the cave walls to make a warmer, more comfortable interior. But, gleaning that the client was attached to the raw stone walls, he came up with his "ship in a bottle" concept, a design which embraced the cave's rustic nature while also subverting it. This meant inserting into the cave space a self-contained structure composed of warm natural woods, glass, and steel. But first, some of the "cave-i-ness" of the cave had to be neutralized.

"The first order of business when we came out here," says Greenlee, "was to work with a civil engineer to drain the water out and devise a plan to keep it from filling back up." The cave's existing lining was not water tight. After pumping out the standing water, the Clayton Korte team devised a water removal system with a central drain pipe that cantilevers out underground beyond the cave mouth to conduct runoff water downhill hundreds of feet away. Over the central drain pipe the concrete slab floor was laid. Around the floor's perimeter, side drains were buried underneath a surface of exposed gravel, allowing any moisture seeping in via the cave walls to percolate down and out.

Korte's "ship in the bottle" structure created a warm, habitable interior space while keeping its wooden walls out of contact with the potentially wet cave walls. A series of windows exposes the stone walls, highlighting the tension between nature and civilization.

The prow of the ship is a comfortable tasting lounge centered around a long island table custom-made from two giant, single cypress planks salvaged from fallen trees on the ranch. They further the connection between the interior and exterior property. The drop ceiling conceals a little attic that houses the mechanical systems, including air conditioning that keeps the room at 75º F. Marked by a tasteful interplay of materials, the room is texturally complex. Douglas fir slats over acoustic fabric line the ceiling. The walls consist of everything from the raw cave sides and board-formed concrete fronts to warmly contrasting mixed-grain and ebonized white oak panels and cabinets. The dark countertop houses a sink, warming oven, dishwasher, and several drawers, while the island conceals a wine fridge to chill bottles.

Floor-to-ceiling thermally broken glazing at the rear separates the lounge space from the wine cellar, putting the wine collection on full display. On the lounge side, an elegant little restroom is enclosed in a cube of contrastingly dark, ebonized oak. The bathroom is outfitted in similar fashion to the rest of the building with warm white oak, steel, and one exposed cave wall.

The drop ceiling of the lounge does not continue into the storage area, which opens up completely to the 18-foot vaulted roof of the cave. The cellar's interior walls are reminiscent of a library, but instead of containing book-lined shelves, oak bins house bottles of wine for storage and display. At the rear, a subtle door opens to an unfinished area for extra storage, mechanicals, and potential expansion of the cellar, should the client need it. This back cellar has self-contained climate control set to the optimal 55º F for wine storage.

Lighting was a major consideration in a naturally dark space. Clear overhead illumination—a necessity in wine evaluation—is supplied by drop lights in both rooms. In the rear cellar room, the voluminous overhead vault is accentuated by a modern custom fixture around which naked bulbs and their wires are dangled to an almost spiderweb like effect. Cave walls on both sides, in contrast, are lit from underneath by hidden fixtures, providing a warm effulgence.

Wine cellars are traditionally dank places, all the better for the aging bottles, which appreciate cool, dark, humid places. Architects, on the other hand, love nothing more than airy spaces, natural light, and vibrant natural surroundings. So how do architects approach a wine cave? Brian Korte, Cam Greenlee, and the Clayton Korte team memorably created a design that harnesses myth and mystery, subverts expectations, and embraces natural contrasts in materials and surfaces. Human beings are preternaturally intrigued by caves and the partially concealed, stealth entrance only feeds that imagination. Its smooth glass portal and lofty wooden door speak to modernity, but the tangle of encroaching natural vegetation on the hillside make it seem as if it's been there forever. We are beckoned in down an almost primitive staircase into the embrace of an almost ritualistic courtyard. But the mixture of textures and materials pull us inside to a bright, cozy interior filled with warm woods and clean lines. Yet the memory of the experience of entrance never leaves us. It is a profound effect that to the visitor will become as memorable as the first lines from a very famous novel:

"In a hole in the ground there lived a Hobbit. Not a nasty, dirty, wet hole … nor yet a dry, bare, sandy hole with nothing in it to sit down on or to eat: it was a hobbit-hole, and that means comfort."

Site Context

Images by **Brodie Kerst**

The Texas Hill Country is known for its endless open skies and rolling landscape marked by limestone outcroppings and cliffs. The grand oak, juniper, and cypress trees dot the hills while wide meadows of native grasses and blankets of springtime wildflowers fill the spaces in between. It is an arid climate yet when conditions allow, natural springs fed by vast aquifers provide respite for plants, animals, and people.

The region has a long heritage of ranching and building traditions adapted to maximize local resources, shade, and cool breezes. Small towns settled in the nineteenth century introduced German building traditions focused on functionality and readily available natural materials like limestone and timber, allowing the buildings to easily blend into the landscape.

Looking east from the Hill Country Wine Cave, limestone cliffs rise above the water's edge lined with bald cypress trees and long grasses. The cliffs are steep and formidable in appearance.

Existing Conditions

Images by **Brian Korte FAIA**

Subterranean wine storage is a sophisticated art dating back to seventeenth century France. The Hill Country Wine Cave builds on these traditions while also adapting to the unique setting of Central Texas. The clients had long desired a space for enjoying their wine collection on their ranch and endeavored to create a cave, burrowing a tunnel more than 75 feet deep into a limestone cliff at a river's edge.

Thus, the wine cave was designed in the context of an existing, excavated cave with dimensional parameters already established. The intent was to safely and beautifully create a wine lounge and cellar within established constraints—recognizing that the existing excavation was neither water tight nor designed for this intent. Despite the logistical and technical challenges, building in a cave offers an extremely unique opportunity to leverage resilience for longevity while minimally impacting the environment.

The textured shotcrete liner forms the entirety of the cave shell. As an existing condition, the design team left this protective barrier in place.

Design Process

Early Concept Design

With the initial design concepts, a sense of hidden refuge became a guiding element of the design. Concealing the cave from the river nearby and integrating it into the hillside were explored with an earthen roof that stepped down on the exterior, but opened up to the full height on the interior. Seamlessly blending into the landscape and sitting quietly, the cave was to be an experience of discovery upon approach, and once inside, a light, intimate interior would unfold and embrace guests.

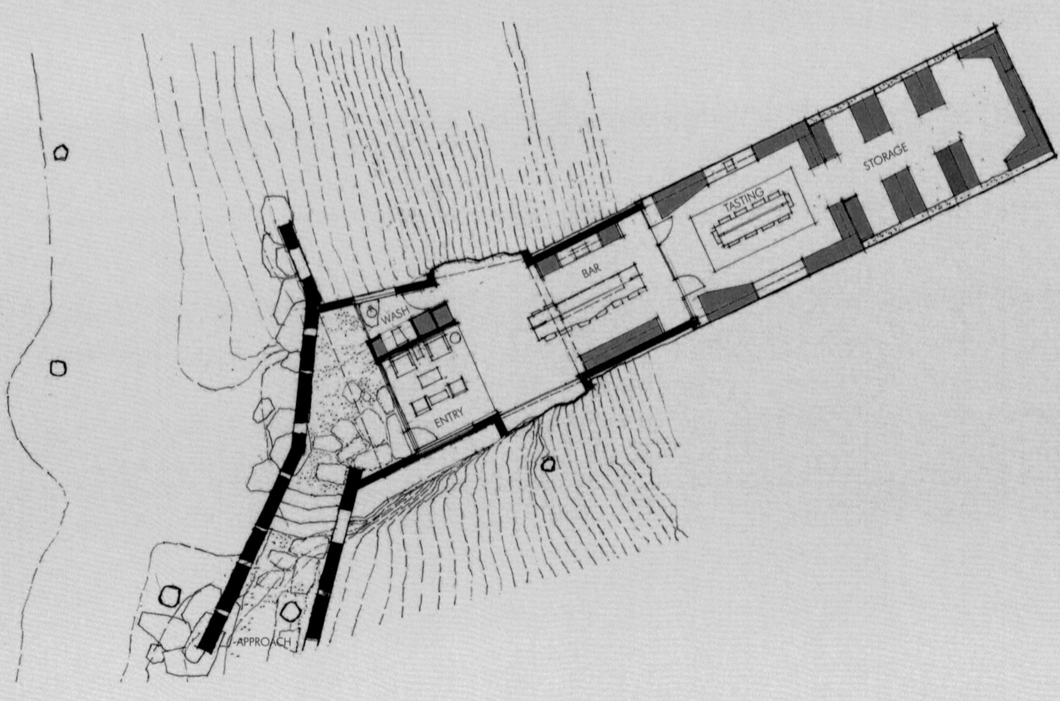

Final Concept Design

As the concept evolved, restraint and rigor led ultimately to a design that allowed the Hill Country Wine Cave to become a stealth insert into the hillside—a nonbuilding, perfectly integrated into the limestone cliff and cascades of green vines. Essentially a delicate wooden module, the wine cave slides into the volume of the excavation, avoiding physical interaction with the cave walls. It is supported by a concrete bulkhead effectively shouldering loose limestone at the cave mouth and providing a predictable surface to wed the wooden insert.

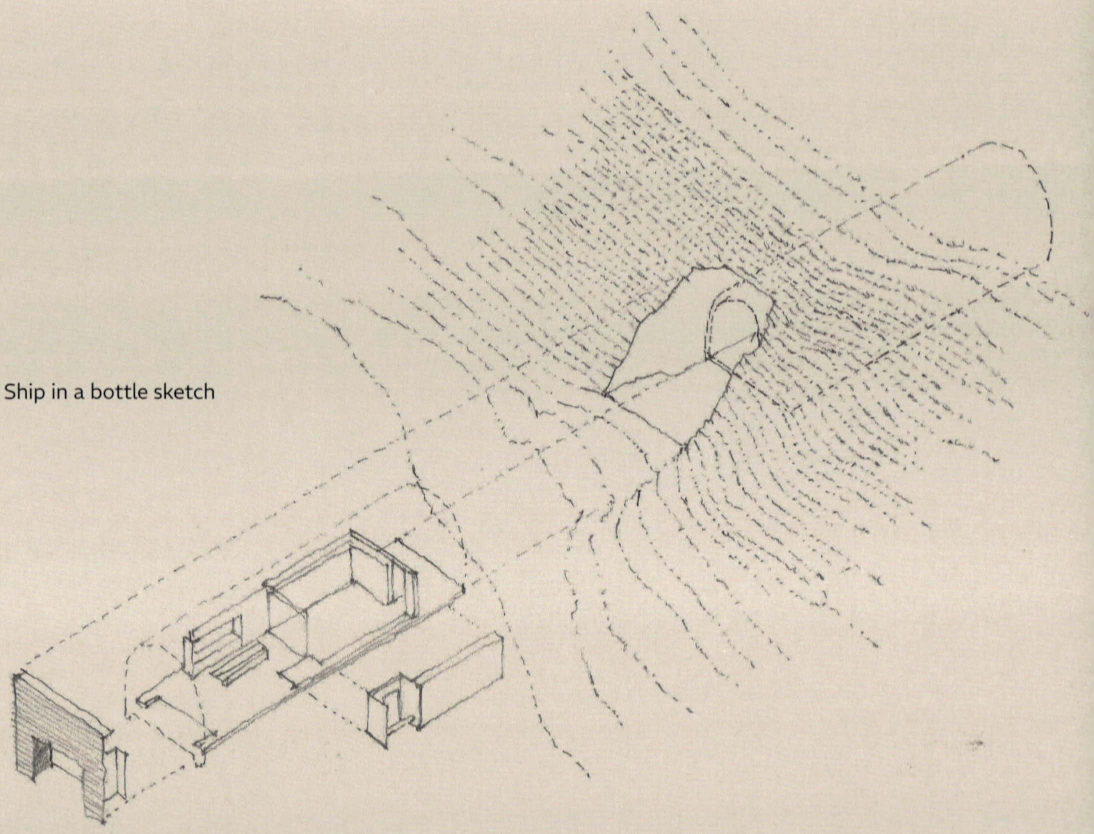

Ship in a bottle sketch

"Like a ship in a bottle, the components of the wood insert are intentionally left away from the existing cave shell, designed to be adaptable by providing flexibility to expand storage over time."

— Brian Korte FAIA

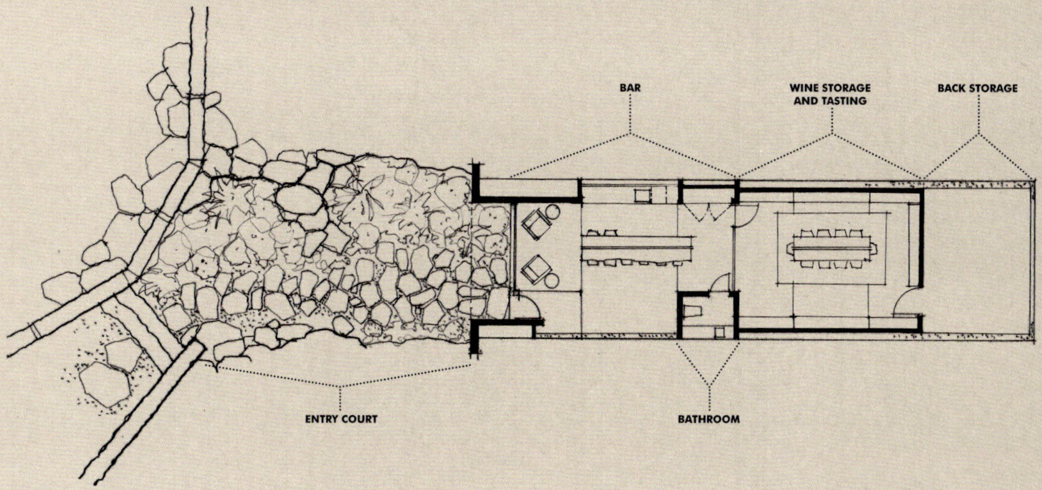

Final concept plan layout

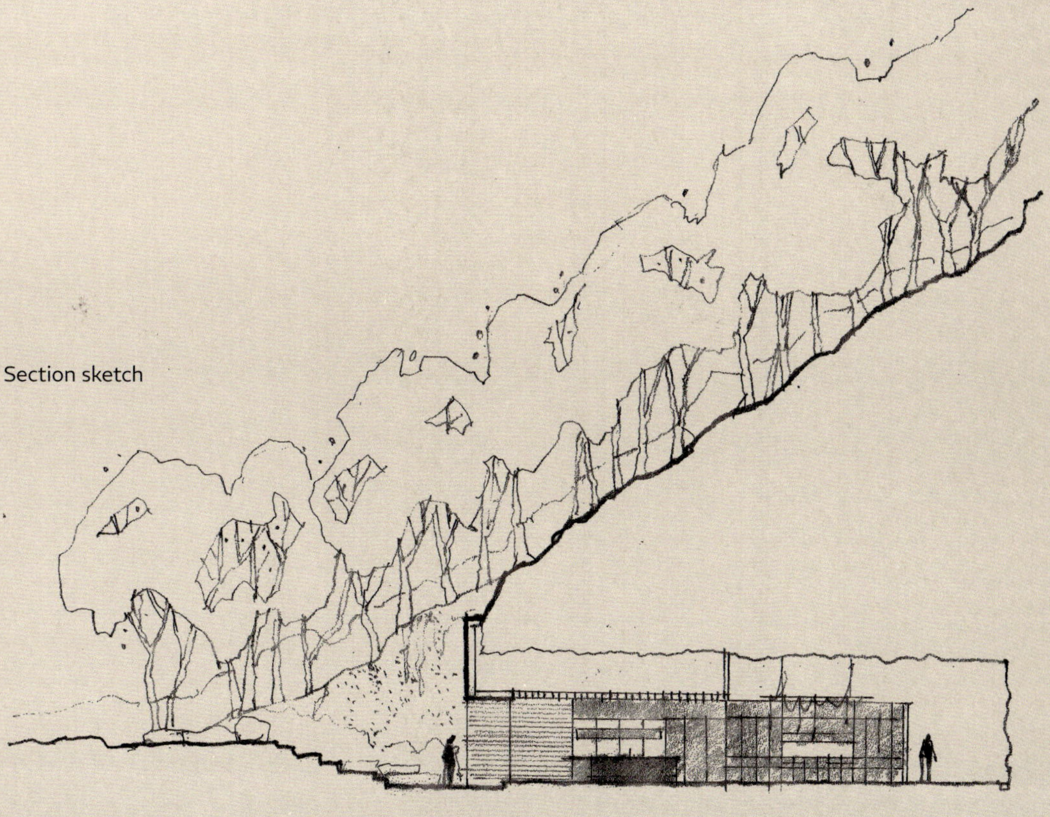

Section sketch

Hill Country Wine Cave **Clayton Korte**

Three dimensionally mapping the excavation's surface and volume created a digital twin of the existing cave. With this accurate "topography," the design team easily fit the wood insertion into the existing and irregular profile of the stone hillside.

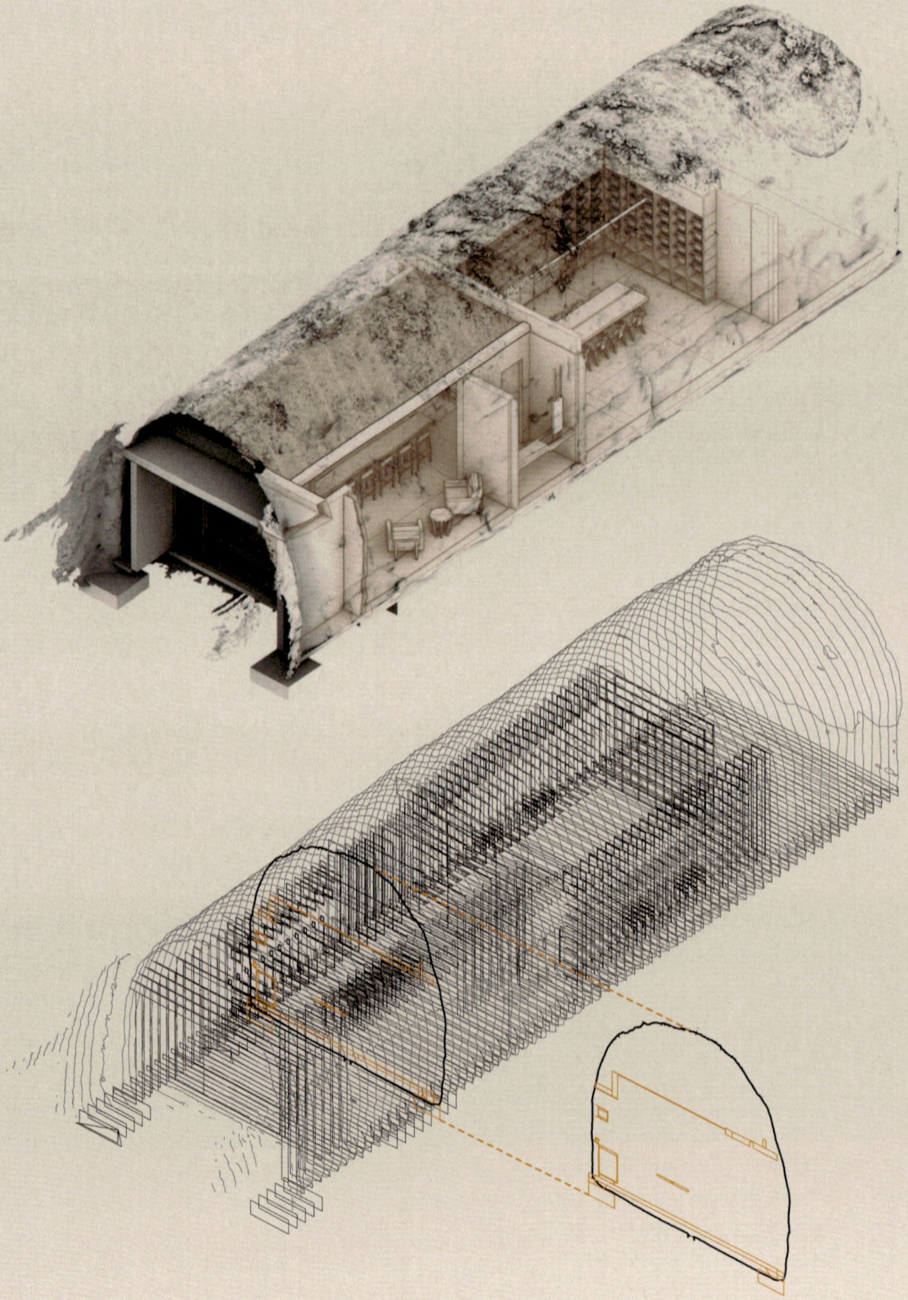

In plan, the space is organized to take full advantage of the natural properties of the cave. The lounge welcomes guests to an inviting and intimate interior, while the cellar is positioned deeper into the excavated volume to provide a more stable and protected environment for the wine collection. By carefully manipulating the solids and voids of the wooden-box, the cave is concealed and revealed to the occupant, leveraging the positive qualities of subterranean construction.

Hill Country Wine Cave **Clayton Korte**

"The project is an instrument. It is a tool or museum that not only provides the utility of proper preservation of wine, but also provides a privileged perspective to the occupant."

— **Camden Greenlee AIA**

Presentation Graphics

Profoundly connected to the site, the Hill Country Wine Cave sits just off the river's edge tucked into the hillside; it is an intimate unassuming experience on the ranch. The sunken exterior entry court reveals a bit of mystery as it provides just a glimpse of what lies within. Heavy limestone boulders, collected from the excavation, and lush vegetation further camouflage the entry to the mouth of the cave.

Simple, yet rich, domestic materials were chosen for practicality, proximity, and for minimal maintenance. Inside, a study of white oak, both raw and ebonized, mixes with vertical grain Douglas fir to panel the walls and dropped ceilings as a warm contrast to more rugged concrete and stone surroundings. With over 80 vertical feet of geology above, the cellar is surrounded by white oak casework providing storage for an ever-expanding private collection of 4,000 bottles.

0 10 50 100

0 2 10

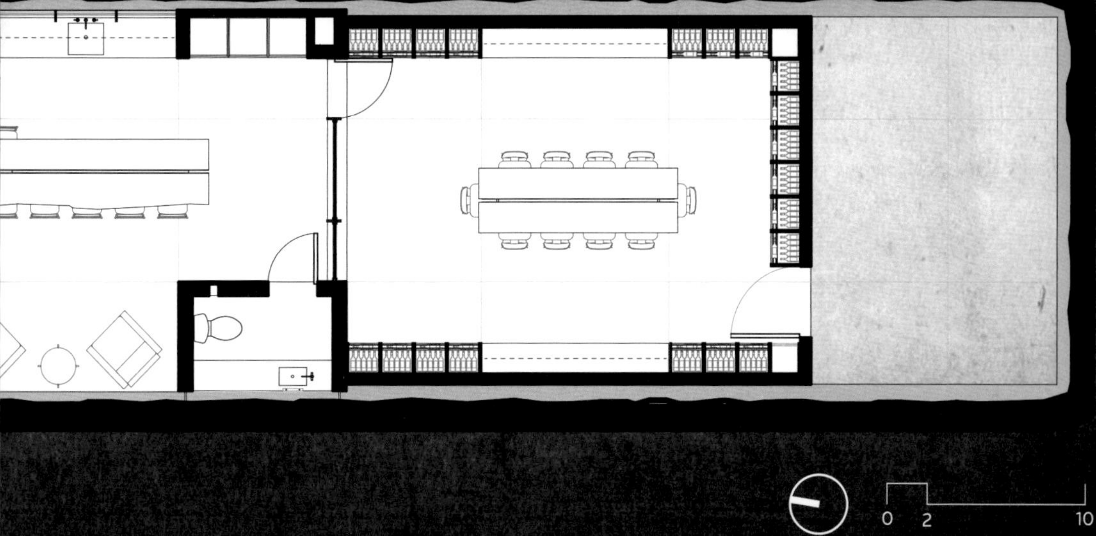
0
2
10

Construction Process

The existing cave opening was a loose formation of irregular limestone surfaces. Exposure and vegetation revealed fractures in the face above the opening that needed to be stabilized and the interior space required a regular surface from which to build. It followed that a strong concrete bulkhead was needed to create such a transition between existing irregularities and a predictable surface. Concrete is flexible and resilient. It molds easily to the surfaces that define it, allowing it to marry equally to the irregular surfaces of the limestone and the regular wood formwork. When it cures, it becomes rigid and durable, able to endure the harsh climate of Texas and protect the delicate interior.

The texture created by board-forming references rhythms of the interior wood paneling and creates a dynamic surface on which daylight may dance. As the concrete ages, variations in exposure will form a spectrum of patina that more clearly reveals the unique circumstances of the bulkhead. The conditions of its position will be, in some poetic sense, visible on its face.

Standing as a silent sentry at the face of the cave, the concrete bulkhead resolves some of the greatest challenges of building in such conditions and lends the kind of grace demanded by such a beautiful landscape.

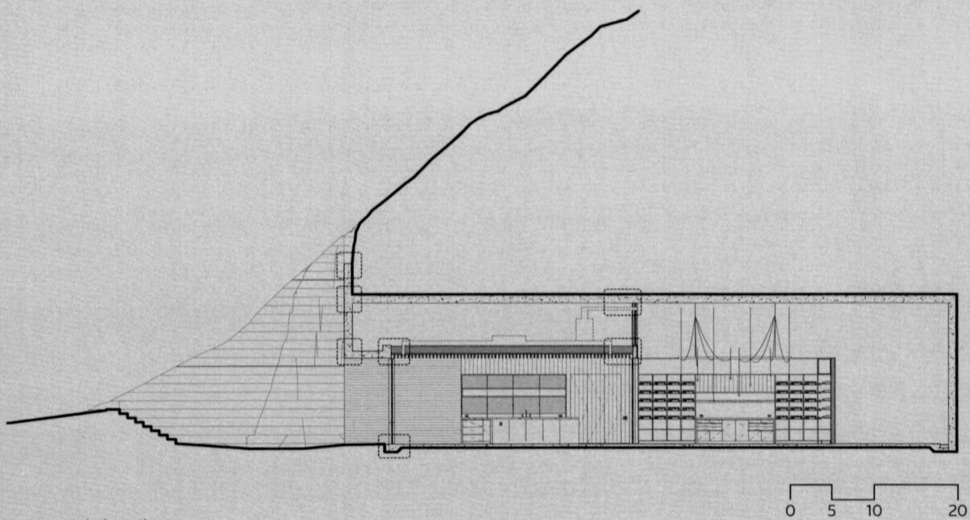

Enlarged detail

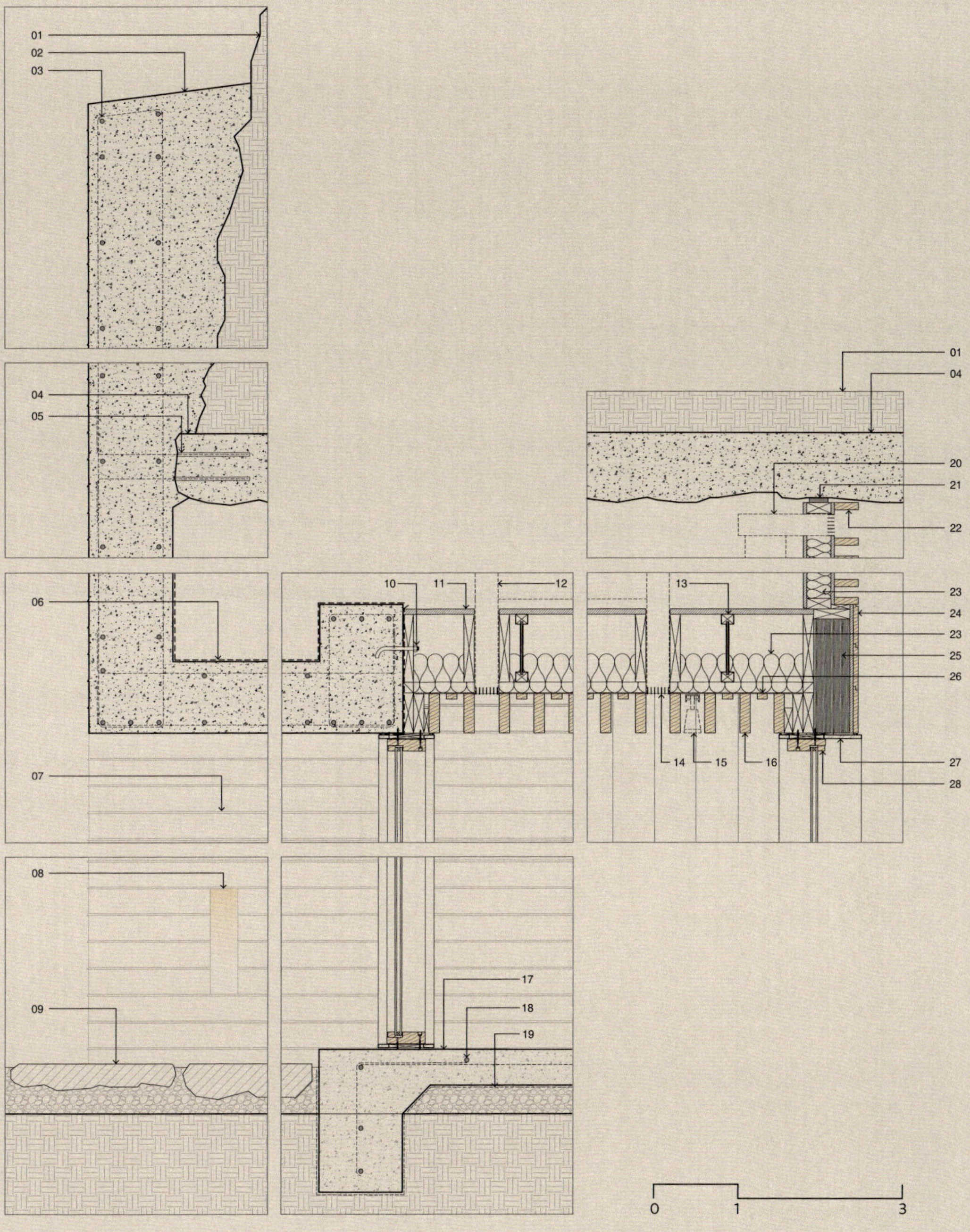

Detail section front

01 Existing hillside. / 02 Existing shotcrete cave shell. / 03 Linear strip light to graze across surface of cave. / 04 1/4" board-formed concrete gap aligned with floor and ceiling. / 05 Paralam wood beam. / 06 Douglas fir tongue-and-groove wall panel - clear finish. / 07 Solid wood entry door - beyond. / 08 1/8" steel plate trim - ebonzied finish. / 09 Douglas fir ceiling slat - clear finish. / 10 Plywood mechanical equipment platform. / 11 Acoustic batt insulation. / 12 Recessed mono-point track light. / 13 White oak tongue-and-groove wall panel - clear finish. / 14 Steel window frame for insulated glazing. / 15 White oak floating shelf. / 16 16 GA sliding steel doors in 1/8" saw kerf. / 17 Recessed linear LED strip light. / 18 1/4" steel plate backsplash - ebonized finish. / 19 Honed black granite countertop. / 20 Welded steel angle and plate support for cantilevered wood island top. / 21 Cypress wood island top with live edge - salvaged from site. / 22 Steel angle foot rest - ebonized finish. / 23 Concrete slab with hard-trowel finish. / 24 Continuous underslab vapor barrier. / 25 Sloped PVC drain pipe for water intrusion. / 26 Sloped utility trough cut into cave floor.

The interior of the cave presented its own challenges. The existing shotcrete liner, made by spraying concrete to the limestone surface, formed the structural shell of the cave. It holds the surrounding limestone in place, but it lacks waterproofing and is an irregular surface. For these reasons the interior wood structure is held away from the cave walls, supported entirely on a floating concrete slab. Should water intrude into the space, it will drip harmlessly down the face of the cave wall into a perimeter gravel border that leads to a central trench drain flowing with gravity to daylight at the exterior.

The strategy of separation from the cave walls allows wet things to be wet, and dry things to stay dry. It expanded the material repertoire to include delicate wood finishes. Clear Douglas fir slats with acoustic fabric backing line the ceiling of the lounge. Clear and ebonized white oak panels line the walls providing warmth and contrast to the rougher exterior and board-formed concrete walls.

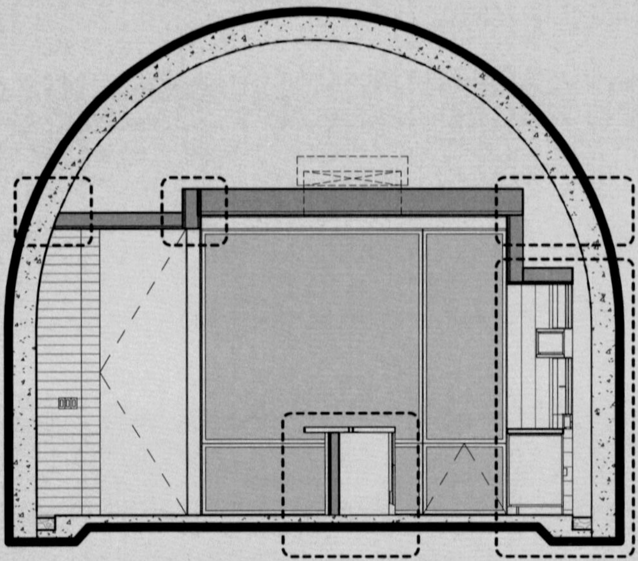

Transverse building section

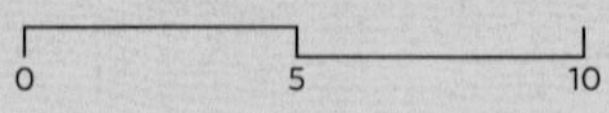

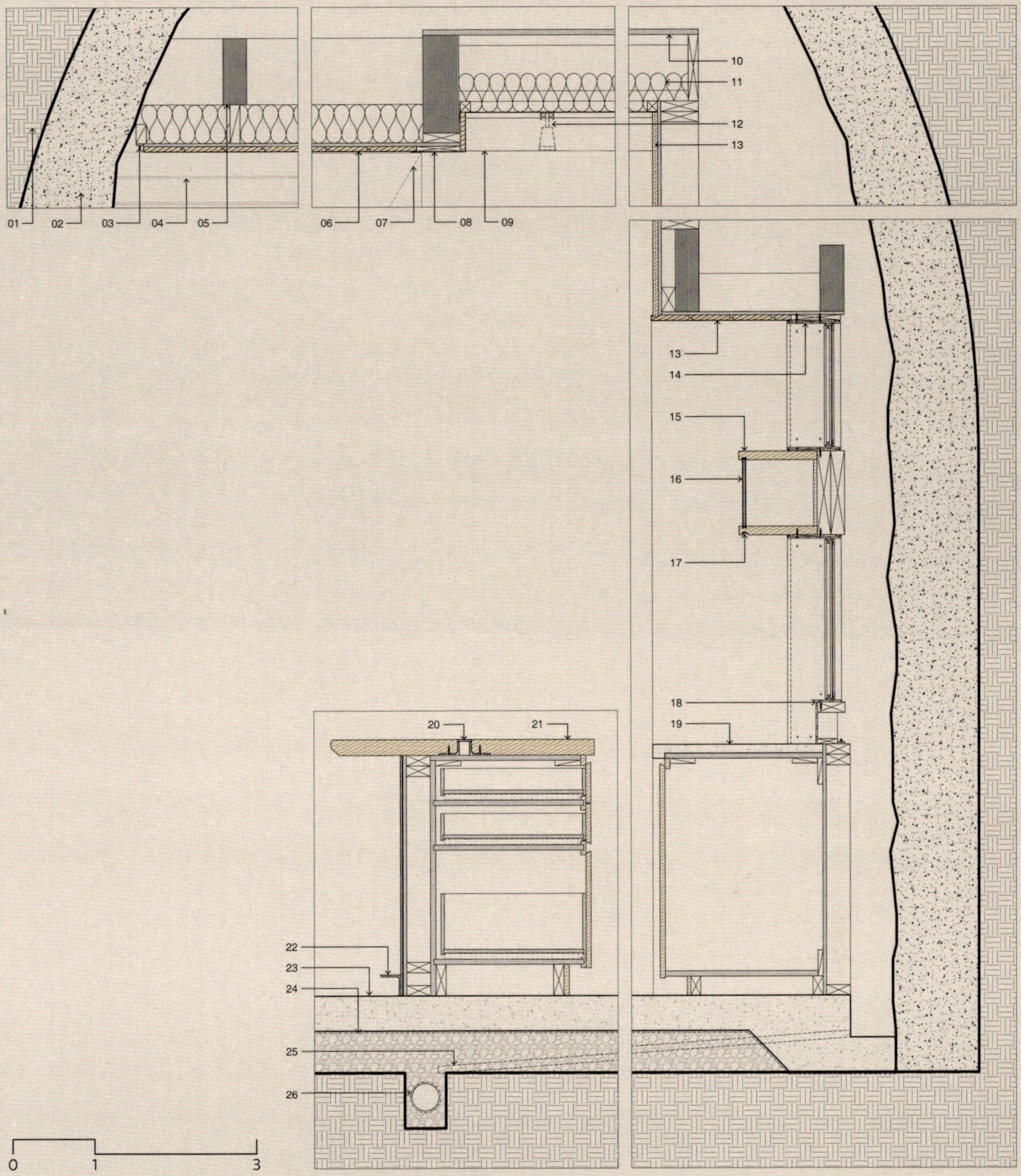

Detail section bar

01 Existing hillside. / 02 Concrete bulkhead - poured against front face of cave. / 03 Concrete reinforcement. / 04 Existing shotcrete cave shell. / 05 Epoxy grouted dowels into existing concrete shell. / 06 Waterproof membrane trough, shed to drainage at sides of cave. / 07 1/4" board-formed concrete gap aligned with floor and ceiling. / 08 Integrated concrete ghost light. / 09 Flagstone pavers set in gravel - sourced from site / 10 Stainless steel concrete anchor. / 11 Plywood mechanical equipment platform. / 12 Supply air duct and grille. / 13 Engineered wood ceiling joist. / 14 Return air duct and grille. / 15 Recessed mono-point track light. / 16 Douglas fir ceiling slat - clear finish. / 17 Concrete slab with hard-trowel finish. / 18 Steel reinforcement. / 19 Continuous underslab vapor barrier. / 20 Supplemental fresh air and conditioned air supply duct and grille. / 21 Compressible seal between framing and cave wall. / 22 Douglas fir wall slats - ebonized finish. / 23 Acoustic batt insulation. / 24 White oak tongue and groove wall panel - ebonized finish. / 25 Paralam wood beam. / 26 Black acoustic fabric between ceiling slats and structure. / 27 Thermally broken steel window trim - ebonized finish. / 28 Custom white oak insulated glazing.

Detail Process

Rich, well-crafted materials form the essence of the interior. Custom millwork details including special steel components like the sandblasted stainless steel sink are opportunities to highlight craft, giving the project its soul. Salvaged cedar slabs, used for the island and vanity tops, reinforce the connection of the project to the legacy of the ranch, while also giving a felled tree a new life as an act of renewal and respect.

Valuing the integration of designer and producer is an essential aspect of reaching authenticity in the project since materials and how they were made, or carefully cut and assembled, serve as a daily reminder of the craftsperson's hand, or perhaps more subtly, a direct connection to our natural environment.

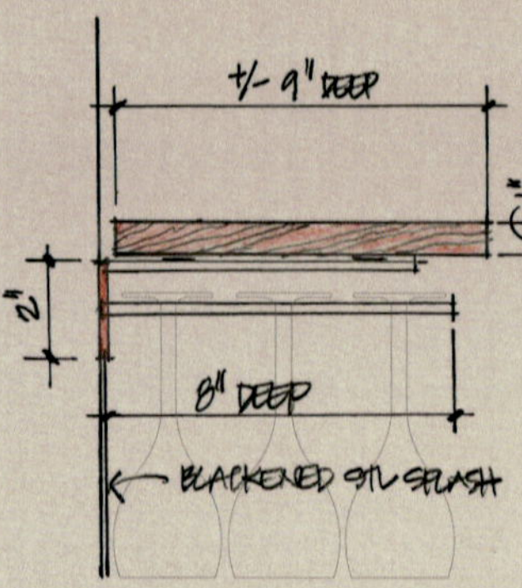

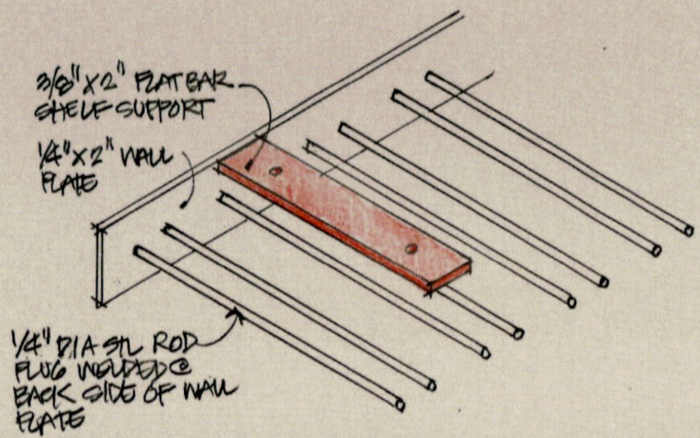

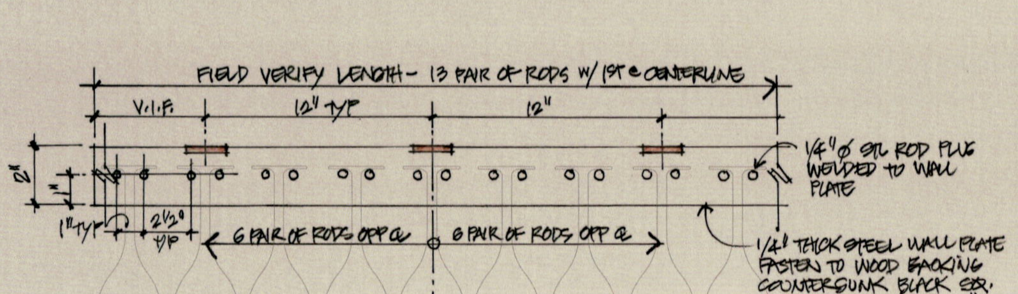

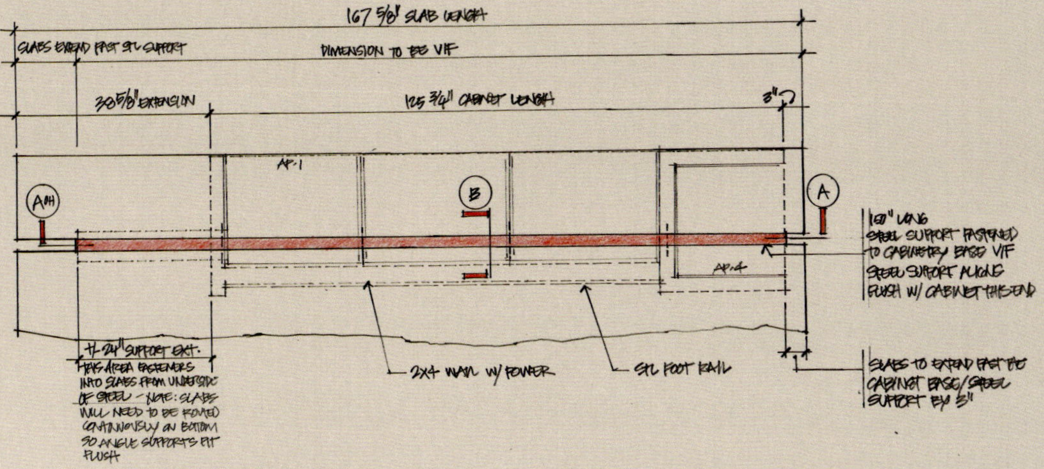
167 5/8" SLAB LENGTH
SLABS EXTEND PAST STL SUPPORT
DIMENSION TO BE VIF
38 5/8" EXTENSION
125 3/4" CABINET LENGTH
3"
AP.1
AP.4
A
B
+/-24" SUPPORT EXT.
2X4 WALL W/ POWER
STL FOOT RAIL
SLABS TO EXTEND PAST THE CABINET BASE/STEEL SUPPORT BY 3"

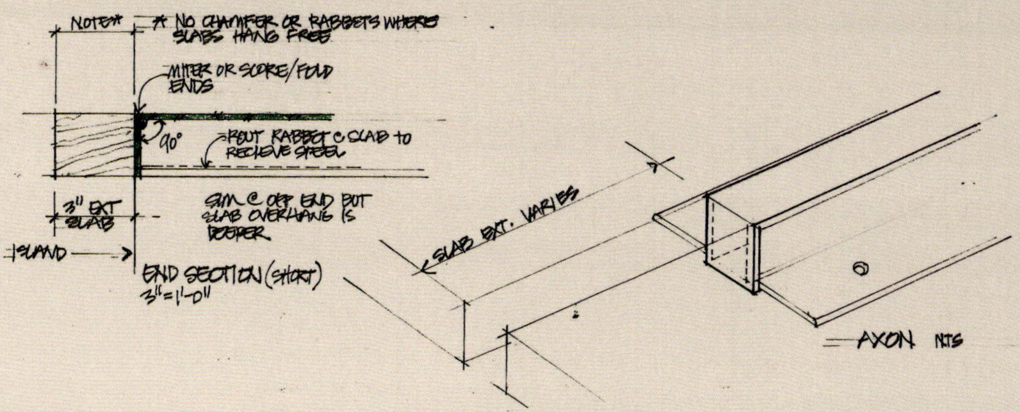
NOTE:* * NO CHAMFER OR RABBETS WHERE SLABS HANG FREE
MITER OR SCORE/FOLD ENDS
90°
ROUT RABBET @ SLAB TO RECIEVE STEEL
3" EXT SLAB
SIM @ OPP END BUT SLAB OVERHANG IS DEEPER
ISLAND
END SECTION (SHORT)
3"=1'-0"
SLAB EXT. VARIES
AXON NTS

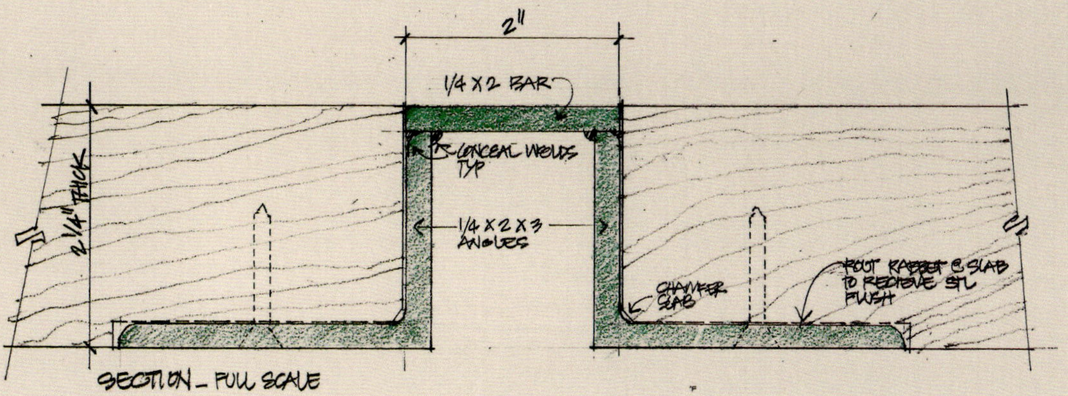
2"
1/4 X 2 BAR
CONCEAL WELDS TYP
2 1/4" THICK
1/4 X 2 X 3 ANGLES
CHAMFER SLAB
ROUT RABBET @ SLAB TO RECIEVE STL FLUSH
SECTION _ FULL SCALE

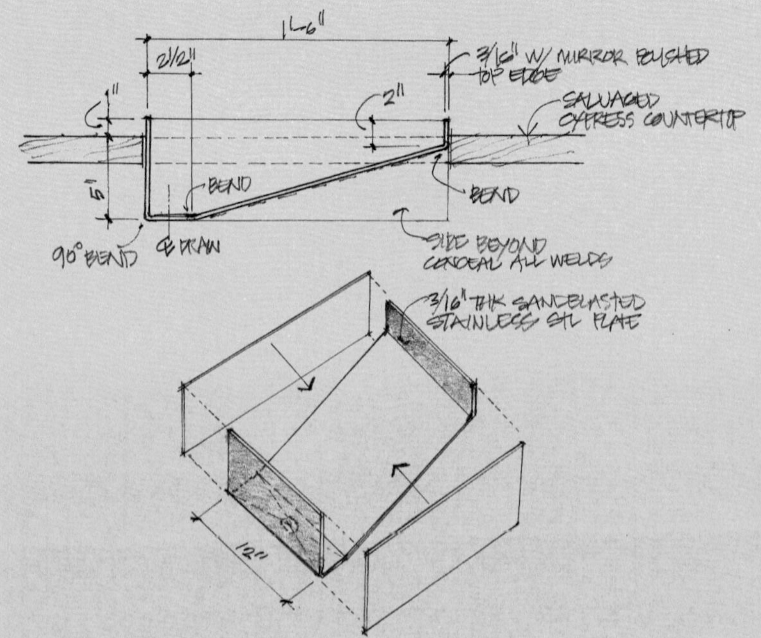

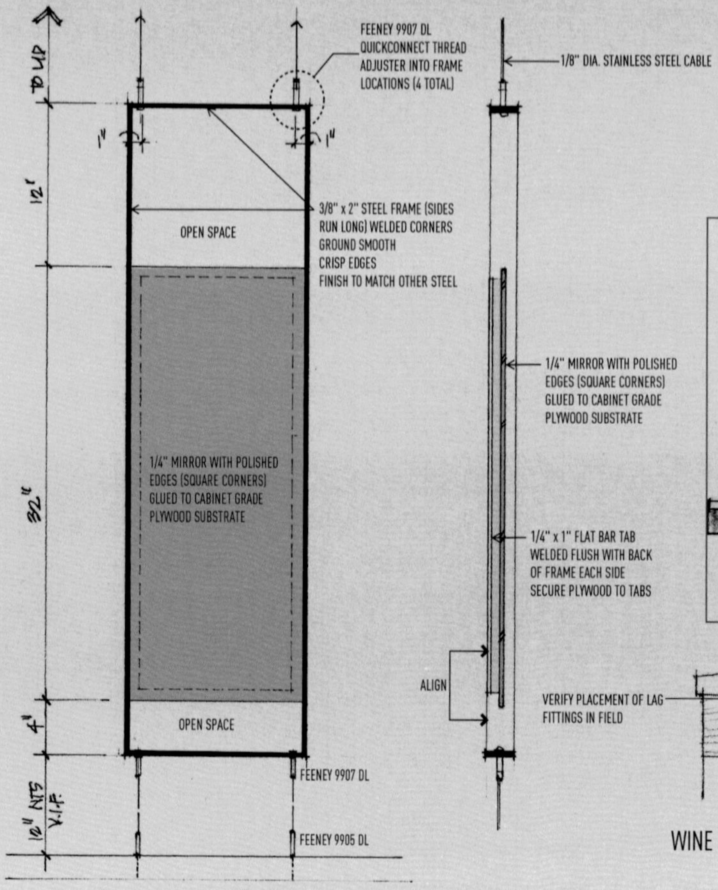

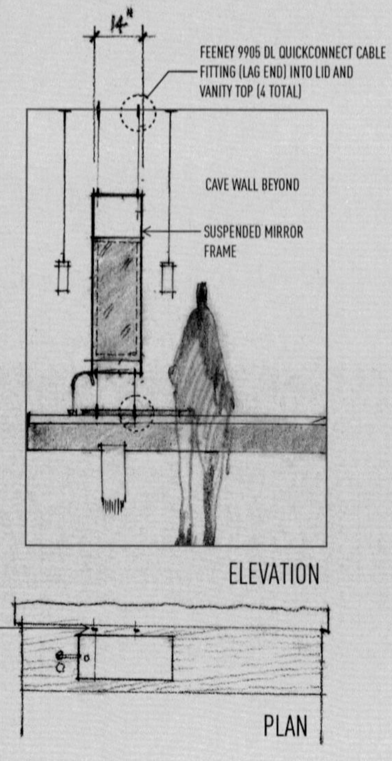

WINE CAVE_BATH MIRROR DETAILS

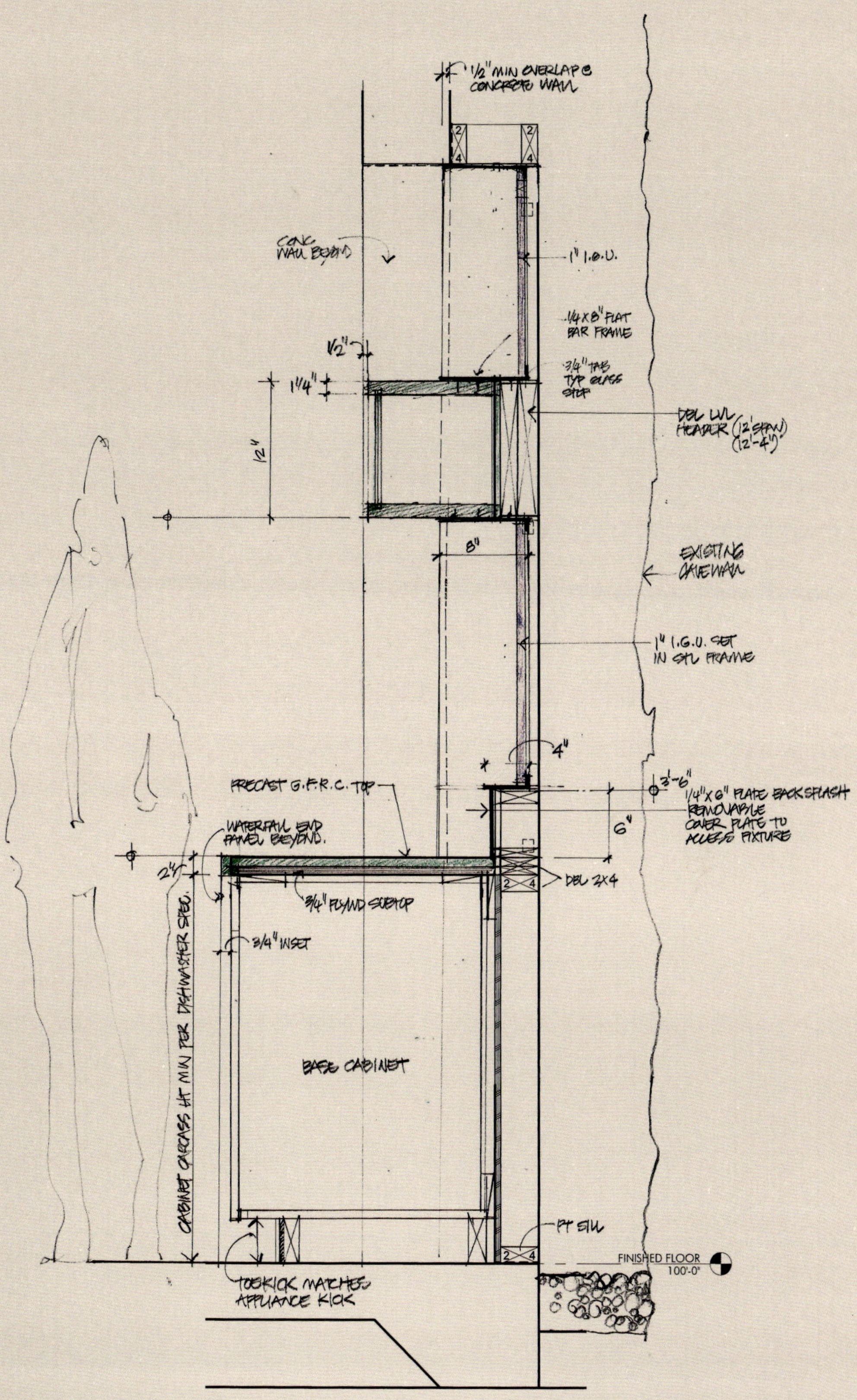
1/2" MIN OVERLAP @ CONCRETE WALL
CONC WALL BEYOND
1" I.G.U.
1/4 X 8" FLAT BAR FRAME
3/4" TAB TYP GLASS STOP
1/2"
1 1/4"
12"
DBL LVL HEADER (12' SPAN) (12'-4")
8"
EXISTING CAVE WALL
1" I.G.U. SET IN STL FRAME
4"
PRECAST G.F.R.C. TOP
3'-6"
1/4" X 6" PLATE BACKSPLASH REMOVABLE COVER PLATE TO ACCESS FIXTURE
6"
WATERFALL END PANEL BEYOND.
2 1/4"
DBL 2X4
3/4" PLYWD SUBTOP
3/4" INSET
BASE CABINET
CABINET CARCASS HT MIN PER DISHWASHER SPEC.
PT SILL
FINISHED FLOOR
100'-0"
TOEKICK MATCHES APPLIANCE KICK

10' interior concrete wall must maintain clearance above wall to accommodate sill plate and 9.5" ceiling joist

16" to cave floor
22" to cave floor

FF is 16" above existing cave floor
12" Bulkhead wall

Bobcat

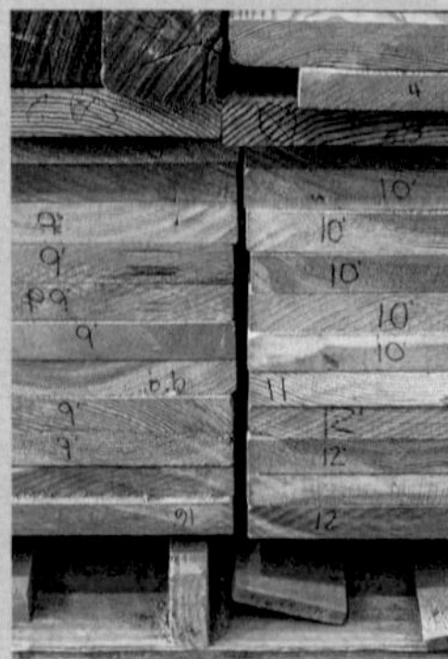

The Cave

"Buildings can partner with a beautiful setting, remaining subservient and quiet, while carrying their own elegance as stewards of the place they are in. Embedding this space into the hillside contributes value to this larger environment by appearing as a non-building, and as a stealth destination that calls little attention to itself."

— Brian Korte FAIA

"This sense of prospect and refuge as you approach and eventually enter the cave is a central tenet of the design. It invites you in and maintains a sense of subterranean occupation without the overwhelming environmental conditions that might make one seek to leave. In this way, the cave can be appreciated from the safety of the interior space in the same way stars can be appreciated from the relative safety of Earth."

— Camden Greenlee AIA

"Vineyard projects allow us to create buildings within the convergence of distilled design, regional ecology, resiliency, and ingenuity. The design takes a step back and lets the natural landscape be the star of the show."

— **Brian Korte FAIA**

"Craft, after all, is the soul of architecture: it is the touch of the hand, the unshakable human quality that adds grace and dignity to a project. It enriches all of Clayton Korte's work."

— **Canan Yetmen**

Hill Country Wine Cave **Clayton Korte**

Hill Country Wine Cave **Clayton Korte**

MASSOLINO

LE MACCHIOLE
LE MACCHIOLE

"The wine cave is the perfect example of our design ethos in action. We strive to make site-specific, architectural interventions that become so much a part of their context, it is hard to imagine them not being there. The unique challenges of building in a cave demand this type of sensitivity."

— **Brian Korte FAIA**

On Inevitability and Character

by Canan Yetmen

In storytelling and narrative, the best endings are ones that are both surprising and inevitable. This insight from Aristotle has held true for centuries because, well, it works. Inevitability, however, is the result of layers of careful crafting of character within the context of plot, circumstance, and setting. It puts a fictional person in a conundrum to see how they react. Story is built, piece-by-piece, using elements that may not always be visible but are definitely palpable. It relies on authenticity. If a writer makes a character do something that goes against their values simply to help get the story to the end, the reader will hear a loud record scratch and feel tricked. The ending hasn't been earned.

Authenticity, inevitability, and surprise are written into the DNA of Clayton Korte's work. Each project embodies a compelling, and ultimately deeply satisfying, design story that closely considers the truth of its context, function, and circumstance, establishing a throughline between what is and what can be. Much like building a character, the architecture seems to ask, What is here to work with? It might be an existing structure, the remnants of a historic wall, the stripped-down infrastructure of an old warehouse, a faraway vista across rolling hills, or the rugged outcropping along a riverbank.

Kingsbury Commons at Pease Park - Austin, Texas

These characteristics of the existing conditions hold the key to what happens next. The architecture doesn't impose itself on these circumstances, rather it responds with honesty and integrity, picking up the thread of the story of place in a way that makes the outcome both inevitable and surprising.

Clayton Korte's stated mission is to exalt the human experience through design. Elevating the experiences of habitation, relaxation and entertainment; of work and labor; and the activities of daily life expands to embrace a larger continuum where architecture doesn't just enhance our lives, it contributes to our keeping of time and understanding of place. By building—literally and figuratively—on what came before, celebrating the established fabric, enriching it in the present, and pushing it into new contexts, it doesn't just connect us, the users, to those stories. It makes us participants.

Deep Roots

One commonality in the work is the clear commitment to making and building, an ethos that respects the experience of process—the layering of the story—to reach the best final outcome. Another is the embrace of the opportunities presented by all types of buildings, not just the high profile, well-financed ones. Hill Country Wine Cave dramatically embodies this attention to the multi-layered act of balancing the technical challenges with the expression of beauty and deference to its place. Clayton Korte's full portfolio of diverse projects of varying scales, levels of visibility and user types is the product of the same attention and respect as markers of a shared history, community, and even identity.

In a project like the Saxum Vineyard Equipment Barn in Paso Robles, California, a potential throwaway building type is elevated to an expression that honors the functions of shelter and protection and dignifies the experience, grounding the structure firmly in the place and time where it belongs. Salvaged industrial materials create a structure—an "armature" in the firm's parlance—that not only houses the winery's farming equipment, but also supports laminated glass

Saxum Vineyard Equipment Barn - Paso Robles, California

Saxum Vineyard Equipment Barn - Paso Robles, California

Saxum Vineyard Equipment Barn - Paso Robles, California

solar modules that provide most of its power. The in-your-face honesty of a gritty, industrial expression with salvaged materials simply but exquisitely executed nods to the traditional forms that inherently withstand the dry climate. The surprising piece is the deceptively delicate perforated Corten steel scrim that, rather than obscuring the machinery inside, filters it into shadow and solid against the backdrop of light.

The humble barn as building typology lends itself well to a pure design response. If the primary function is to provide shelter for inanimate objects indifferent to the effect of prevailing breezes and dappled light, then the opportunity is to create the moments of surprise in the experience of the people who move in and out of the space. Humans engage with the light and breezes. They reach out to touch the texture of the steel and observe the patination of the materials over time. The simple building with its soaring shed roof that seems only loosely tethered to the grounding structure tells a story of the place where it resides and the purpose it serves in a way that shifts our expectations of utilitarian structures.

The equipment barn stands sentry along entry to the vineyard and establishes the winery's abiding commitment to existing in harmony with the land. The recycled drill-stem pipe structure supports a photovoltaic roof system that offsets more than 100 percent of the winery's power demands. Its design efficiently harnesses cross-ventilation, daylight, and solar energy to eliminate dependence on grid-tied power for both the winery and the vineyard irrigation wells. Pervious gravel paving for all open vehicle storage bays and livestock pens also filters water back through the soil into the watershed.

The seeds of the utility-as-beauty design carry forward

Kingsbury Commons at Pease Park - Austin, Texas

and reappear at the Kingsbury Commons at Pease Park in Austin, Texas. Here, the clear lineage appears in the low-maintenance park support buildings that store equipment and house public restrooms. In the context of the oldest public park in the city, the buildings sidle up to a mix of existing conditions: Civilian Conservation Core-era communal tables, remnants of stone arches, and, somewhat incongruously, a charming 1920s Tudor cottage. Reverse engineering converted the cottage, which formerly contained restrooms, into an intimate, bright and modern event and meeting space that celebrates its structure and allows it to open its doors wide onto a plaza and engage directly with the support buildings, bringing them fully into the fold of the park's activities.

Evoking classic Texas vernacular shapes—shed roofs and dog trot-style breezeways—the grouping creates a composition that encourages park visitors to gather and pause amid the mix of uses that include playground, an events lawn, picnic areas, and walking/biking paths, lifting their presence way beyond their utilitarian function. Like the Saxum Barn, this pair, clad in steel mesh with clerestories and floating shed roofs, act as an infrastructure, this time for the park's landscape architecture, supporting vines and surrounded by native shrubs and grasses, giving the sense that they've been there forever.

The pragmatic relationship to land and landscape is central to life in Texas, where the climate tends to frown upon attempts at gentrifying and softening the edges of the natural order of things. For Clayton Korte, context is always site and site always has a valuable story, even when it's a decommissioned Texaco distribution depot with pair of run-down, graffiti-covered sheet metal warehouses. In their revived incarnation as Cosmic Saltillo, a sustainably minded

Fulldraw Winery - Paso Robles, California

Cosmic Saltillo - Austin, Texas

all-day coffee shop, restaurant, and bar centered around a rambling courtyard, the site looks as though it transformed itself organically. Old, worn, and weathered buildings (the two warehouses were stabilized and gutted to accommodate the bar and taqueria) blend seamlessly with the insertion of a double-height cylindrical tower with vertical steel elements that provides rooftop views of the city skyline. Existing walls were integrated into the perimeter, new murals added in strategic spots, and materials salvaged from the site re-used throughout. The careful orchestration of these elements creates the perfect conditions for the seemingly spontaneous, instinctual landscaping that create this secret-feeling garden for city folk of all ages to enjoy. Here again, the building is a kind of armature for lush greenery that sprouts between buildings, spills onto surfaces, and climbs over walls in a charming impersonation of a natural, inevitable rewilding being kept comfortably at bay.

Working with the Land

It might feel like a wide swing, then, to shift from urban oil depots to more rarified and sophisticated California winery projects. The rolling hills and magnificent vistas of Paso Robles and the Central Coast of California need no enhancement, of course. Placing an agricultural and industrial function in this context runs a real risk of screwing things up. But like the grittier Cosmic project, they have the same task: tell the story of the place by inviting people to experience it in a new way. Wine production is a craft intrinsically connected to its place and the buildings are the physical manifestations of the vintner's ideals, history and identity. California wine country is storied and deeply rooted in the art of making, perfecting, and continuously adapting.

Early work in the wine country included production and storage facilities and tasting rooms for Epoch Estate Wines and Saxum Vineyards, both with significant subterranean elements that embedded the architecture into the land, obscuring the building but celebrating the process of making. Designs for Fulldraw Vineyard and Copia Winery and Tasting Room build on that respect for the land while creating a beautiful place for visitors and workers to interact with it. Both projects celebrate the elegance of sleek, streamlined utility—fermentation and processing functions are front and center—that fosters a conversation among materials, form, and context. The architecture is light-footed and respectful, focused on human-scaled composition and interstitial spaces creating a rhythm of solid and void, push and pull, and balancing shelter and prospect to frame large views and small glimpses of the surrounding landscape. Up close, function and hospitality are on display, but from a distance, buildings retreat into the landscape, leaving it as visually untouched as possible. The architecture is complementary to the land, framing layers of understanding rather than obscuring or imposing itself on it.

The stunning site of the Eureka Retreat and Hotel at Avila Beach overlooking San Luis Obispo Bay demanded the architecture proceed with both caution and acclaim for the surrounding beauty. Giving architectural meaning to the word "retreat," the building is set into a curved ridge, its design following the topography to maximize

Cosmic Saltillo - Austin, Texas

Eureka Retreat + Hotel - Avila Beach, California

Backwards Sky Ranch - Reagan Wells, Texas

Copia Winery and Tasting Room - Paso Robles, California

Eureka Retreat + Hotel - Avila Beach, California

views to the ocean and minimize the impact on the land. Its roof is planted with native grasses making the building virtually invisible from the existing property located up the hill to its north and keeping those views almost untouched. Amenity areas are placed at the front edge to make the most of the breathtaking vistas. Approaching the building from the north, it appears simply as a manicured piece of typography, while from the beach below its painted steel, redwood and concrete palette read as an outcropping in the hill above.

The same restraint appears in the firm's residential work, where the connections to views and landscape play a similar role. In the Texas Hill Country, the Backwards Sky Ranch straddles an open meadow along the banks of the dry Frio River. Its living spaces run parallel to the river along the length of the home and float above the ground floor to afford uninterrupted views. At the south and west, the building is anchored into the ground by hefty stone bastions to allay the effects of the summer sun. The laid-back dog trot plan and gable forms are opened, simplified, and carved out to encourage natural ventilation from air moving across the riverbed and to encourage the owners to move around the house throughout the day as conditions warrant. Time-tested materials, including mortared limestone walls and western red cedar siding, will patina and recede into the color palette of the site.

Knowing Your Place

The Canyon Residence at Wildcat Hollow does a similar balancing act, this time accommodating a challenging and steep site in the hills west of Austin. The plan bookends two living spaces connected by a suspended transparent bridge that mimics the traditional dogtrot form, makes visual connection from the street to the views beyond, and anchors the two volumes that cantilever above the site and outdoor space below. The design, with its recognizable forms extruded and expanded into this site-specific composition, minimizes disturbance to the topography. A subtle butterfly roof reinforces the sense of the home hovering above the tree canopy. Eschewing a showy palette, materials are resilient and robust, and appropriate for the rugged site: a painted steel structure and naturally patinated copper combined with poured-in-place concrete, burnished concrete block and charred Accoya siding that communicate an authentic connection to traditional, elemental construction with deep roots in the region.

This deeply rooted regionalism also informs the firm's rehabilitation and adaptive re-use of historic structures. While interventions into historic contexts can be purely technical or cosmetic, strategic or functional, Clayton Korte embraces these projects as opportunities to open a lively conversation between past and present that lays a path to the future ahead. In projects like the Double B Ranch Lodge in Fredericksburg, Texas, the interventions tend to the structure's historic bones while reinterpreting uses and experiences by introducing new and unexpected, but entirely appropriate, elements. These approaches transform a building that successfully fulfilled its initial purpose but had become anachronous and incongruous with modern life into something fully integrated with our expectations of accommodation and comfort.

At Double B Ranch, an 1865 timber-barn transported by a previous owner from Ohio is rehabilitated as the ranch's lodge, welcoming and accommodating extended family members of multiple generations with all the expected modern amenities. The design removed the cliched markers of traditional ranch design, stripped it down to its essential structure, and strategically concealed 21st-century technology. Updated finishes are combined with lime-washed antique brick, plaster, blackened steel, and contrasting ebonized wood floors. The site-quarried limestone and poplar tree bark shingle siding on the exterior will patina and help return the barn, part of a larger composition of family homestead, cabins, and outdoor spaces, to the land. It expresses the honesty of a building that, with these skillful and unpredictable interventions, will live on. The work reflects an investment beyond the reclamation of a venerable vernacular building but carrying it forward, firmly grounded in the spirit of its origins.

Facing the Inevitable

The ability to see the beauty in a building's bones connects to the firm's fundamental principles of assembly, making, and honesty in craft. The foundation of time-tested gestures informed by history, topography, culture, and climate—the core values of the architecture — undergird the quiet but affecting, even surprising, detail of an artfully crafted joint, a wash of light across a concrete wall, the ripples of a corrugated shed roof against the sky.

Truthful design is a counterbalance to an often fickle and disposable culture eager to discard the worn in favor of the shiny next thing. Like a compelling story, a good building is not obviously linear or cumulative, but continually planting seeds to plan the future, circling back to earlier events, responding to shifting forces, and drawing inspiration from all around. Clayton Korte's architectural narrative leads from the refined, yet gritty equipment barn to the cheerful park structures, through warehouses, wineries and historic homesteads, into thin-edged, sculptural modernist objects and gleaming industrial operations before circling back to a historic barn-turned family-lodge and the retreating hotel assimilated with the land. The continual motion is grounded in truth and always in pursuit of a bigger goal. Sometimes the best move is counterintuitive or maybe it's hewing to the tried-and-true or putting a new spin on an old approach. Along the way outcomes are foreshadowed. Seeds are planted. Outcomes hoped for. Adherence to guiding principles moves the design toward the inexorable ending that only in retrospect is revealed as the only possible outcome.

In Clayton Korte's architecture and interiors, the pieces fall into place in a way we didn't see coming but we know to be true to the building's time and place. The design understands what is there to work with and what is necessary. It knows where to shine—perhaps even dazzle just a little and where to pull back. A threshold to something more than just its function, it engages the senses, delights and moves us, and allows us to join in the telling of the story.

Canyon Residence at Wildcat Hollow - Austin, Texas

Double B Ranch Lodge - Fredericksburg, Texas

Photography Captions

The existing limestone walls are marked by manmade cuts into the cliffside to create the cave and the natural fissures due to the movement of water through the stone over time—both create the textural cave shell.

Native oaks, cedar elms and other hardwoods cover the surrounding hillside.

Carefully coursed boards that lined the concrete formwork of the bulkhead register the recessed step light.

The depressed entry courtyard provides a magical sense of reveal as one approaches.

The cellar is the heart of the cave. It provides storage for an expanding collection of approximately 4,000 bottles as well as a space for entertaining and tasting.

The rhythmic and rough lines of the board-formed concrete mark the entry transitioning from the natural organic lines of the limestone to the refined interior of the wine cave.

Expansive skies with rolling, rocky limestone hills, long grasses, and grand trees define the landscape of the Texas Hill Country.

Existing limestone walls, scarred by the cave excavation, invite new landscape growth and recede once again into the hillside.

Looking east from the Hill Country Wine Cave, limestone cliffs rise above the water's edge lined with bald cypress trees and long grasses. The cliffs are steep and formidable in appearance.

The river banks are dense with vegetation, creating feelings of seclusion and immersion in nature.

The wine cave sits just shy of a bend in the water's edge where two rivers meet. The colors of the sky are amplified throughout the day in the water's reflection.

Solid limestone retaining walls shoulder the earth on either side of the entry.

The hidden cave disappears into the green canopy of its wooded surroundings.

The stealth cave has become so much a part of its greater ranch landscape that it is hard to imagine it not being there.

The depressed entry courtyard provides a magical sense of reveal as one approaches.

A concrete portal effectively restrains the loose limestone at the cave mouth, providing a predictable surface with which to wed the wooden insert. The warmth of the interior space within the hill is carefully revealed to the occupant, leveraging the good qualities of subterranean construction.

A recessed, step light softly illuminates the wine cave entry.

Existing shotcrete-coated walls are left exposed throughout the interior providing contrast to the well-crafted wood finishes.

Salvaged live-edge cedar planks are given a new life as the island bar top.

Camden Greenlee AIA. Contemplation.

A floating white oak shelf spans custom glazing sitting proud of the cave wall.

The smooth, natural texture of the grain patterns of the white oak paneling contrasts with the darker, polished finish of the ebonized walnut base cabinetry and honed slate countertop.

The simple glass and steel entry filters daylight into the interior and provides a visual connection to the outdoors.

Simple elegance characterizes the interior where the rough natural feeling of the cave meets curated, intimate moments.

The rhythm of naturally finished, wood-slat ceiling is refined and tranquil—distinguishing the relaxing interior from the rough texture of the exterior visible beyond the glazing.

Ebonized oak wall paneling on the exterior becomes raw on the interior.

The smooth surfaces of a custom sandblasted, stainless-steel sink and blackened-steel mirror frame juxtapose the rough texture of the exposed cave wall.

A polished nickel deck mount faucet by Watermark Designs flanks the sink.

The custom, sandblasted stainless-steel sink was fabricated by our late friend, the talented master artisan Cactus Max Patino (Jan 2019).

Bringing the craft of custom fabricated wood and steel components together gives the project soul.

Ebonized oak wall paneling and base cabinetry provide contrast to the raw Douglas fir slatted ceiling which manages adjustable lighting and discreet slot air diffusers.

Lit by an inlaid linear LED fixture, blackened steel creates the clean lines of the custom stemware rack and serving bar.

The white oak and blackened steel wine bin storage organizes the collection while also allowing for a curated presentation of the wines.

The cellar is the heart of the cave. It provides storage for an expanding collection of approximately 4,000 bottles as well as a space for entertaining and tasting.

The existing limestone walls are marked by manmade cuts into the cliffside to create the cave.

An elegant, suspended pendant light fixture designed by the architect creates a delicate and playful touch in the vaulted space of the cave.

The sunken entry to the wine cave is slowly becoming part of the hillside again as the cut limestone walls and steps are taken over by new plant growth.

A recessed Sistemalux, ghost light softly illuminates the wine cave entry.

Boulders quarried from the cave excavation mark the flagstone path to the entry garden.

An inviting warm glow of light comes from within the cave.

Glazing is scribe fit to the textured concrete shell, holding the gap between the cave and wood box insert.

Rolling, rocky limestone hills, long grasses, and grand trees define the landscape of the Texas Hill Country.

Photographers

Casey Dunn

Casey Dunn's aesthetic is marked by an inclusion of life within his composition of spaces, a testament to the human element of design. He refined this technique working on both coasts before returning to his hometown of Austin, Texas. Since then, he has settled in and regularly collaborates with the leading designers and creators in the country.

Dunn has photographed six books; *Not Forgotten and Paradox Cove*, in collaboration with Pentagram; the *University of Texas Architectural Guide*, for Princeton Architectural Press; and *Santa Fe Modern, Marfa Modern* and *Texas Made Texas Modern*, all with writer Helen Thompson, for Phaidon Monacelli Press. His work has been featured in local, regional, and national magazines including *Dwell, Architectural Record, Architectural Digest, Icon Design, The New York Times Magazine, Interior Design Magazine*, and *Texas Monthly.*

On Saturdays, Casey can be found working in the garden or watching college football. In the offseason he's probably camping, motorbiking, swimming, or hiking with his wife Sarah and son Jack.

Shannon Korta

Shannon has specialized in architecture photography for almost a decade. She began her career on the west coast, shooting in Washington state, Oregon, and Montana, and is now based in San Antonio, Texas. She has shot a wide variety of projects, from Residential, Hospitality, Ranches, Wineries, Healthcare, Civic, Restaurants, Multi-Family Housing, Education, Spas, Performing Arts, and more. Shannon has a high regard for beauty, craftsmanship, and telling stories.

Brodie Kerst

Videographer Brodie Kerst, trained in architecture and design, holds a deep appreciation for the built environment. Paired with his natural ability for video storytelling, he captures projects and spaces in a light that shows not just how they look, but how they are meant to be experienced.

Authors

Brian Korte FAIA

A native Texan, Brian leads the San Antonio studio and the firm's residential, ranch, and vineyard-related projects currently in California, Hawaii, and Texas. With a passion for authenticity, richness, and well-crafted materials, Brian's work champions the honesty of modernism with a commitment to practical yet artful solutions.

Each project maintains a focus on the convergence of distilled design, regional ecology, ingenuity, and resilience that allows the structures to step back in favor of the surrounding natural landscape.

Paul Clayton AIA LEED AP

In addition to being a skilled architect and designer, Paul is an accomplished entrepreneur who has led Clayton Korte with a disciplined approach since 2005. In his first 15 years as principal, he grew a five-person architecture firm into an interdisciplinary design firm with offices in two cities, and a team of more than 30 professionals.

Paul has always found inspiration in landscapes, as they epitomize the inevitable yet graceful passage of time. He approaches architecture with an eye toward timeless beauty and functionality and his wide-ranging design capabilities span styles.

Camden Greenlee AIA

Cam grew up on a farm in northern Illinois, west of Chicago. After receiving his master's degree in architecture at the University of Illinois, he taught undergraduate design courses as an adjunct professor for four years at his alma mater which honed his understanding of the value of teamwork and design dialogue. His interests in architecture stem from an appreciation for the subtleties of materials, light, and the procession of space.

He is an avid bicycle commuter, personally sponsoring the firm's annual Bike to Work Challenge, and has a deep affinity for music.

Contributors

Tom Kundig FAIA RIBA

Tom Kundig, FAIA, RIBA, has spent over four decades crafting award-winning architecture across six continents as principal / owner and founder of global design firm Olson Kundig. His works spans adaptive reuse developments and hospitality destinations to sports facilities and venues, museums, wineries, private homes, and more. Tom has received some of the world's highest design honors, including more than two dozen AIA National Honor Awards and an Academy Award in Architecture from the American Academy of Arts and Letters. He regularly lectures around the world, and has been named in The Wallpaper* 400 as a "tastemaker" of American culture.

Jordan Mackay

Jordan Mackay is a James-Beard-award-winning journalist. His work on wine, food, and spirits has appeared in *Food & Wine*, *The New York Times*, *Los Angeles Times*, *San Francisco Chronicle*, *Decanter*, and many others. He's the author of nine books, including *Secrets of the Sommeliers* and *The Sommeliers Atlas of Taste* (with Rajat Parr), *Franklin BBQ* (with Aaron Franklin), and *The Maison Premiere Almanac.*

Oscar Riera Ojeda

Oscar Riera Ojeda is an editor and designer based in the US, China, and Argentina. Born in 1966, in Buenos Aires, he moved to the United States in 1990. Since then, he has published over three hundred books, assembling a remarkable body of work notable for its thoroughness of content, timeless character, and sophisticated and innovative craftsmanship. Oscar Riera Ojeda's books have been published by many prestigious publishing houses across the world.

In 2008 he established his current publishing venture, Oscar Riera Ojeda Publishers, a firm with fifteen employees and locations across three continents.

Canan Yetmen

Canan Yetmen is a writer based in Austin, Texas. A former publisher of *Texas Architect* magazine, she works with architects to craft stories that illuminate the value and importance of good design in shaping a better world. She is an honorary member of the Texas Society of Architects and author of three novels.

Project Credits

Location: Texas Hill Country
Area: 1,405 square feet, conditioned
Completion: 2020

Collaborators List
Clayton Korte Design Team
Brian Korte FAIA, Principal
Camden Greenlee AIA, Project Architect
Josh Nieves AIA
Brandon Tharp
Interiors - Clayton Korte
Structural Engineering - Buehler Engineering
Mechanical Engineer - Positive Energy
Civil Engineer - Intelligent Engineering Services
Lighting Design - Studio Lumina
Landscape Design - Clayton Korte
General Contractor - Monday Builders

Acoustics
Boyd Rib FR acoustic fabric
Appliances
InSinkErator, Miele, Perlick, Sub Zero/Wolf
Architectural Concrete
Dash Concrete
Architectural Metals
Cactus Max Fine Metal Artwork,
Fasone & Associates
Cabinetry Fabrication
Monday Builders
Framing
Anthony Forest Products, Boise Cascade
Glazing
Vitro Architectural Glass Solarban 60 IGU,
Fasone & Associates
Hardware
Rocky Mountain Hardware, SIMONSWERK,
Saint Louis Design, Dorma, Deltana, IVES
Lighting Fixtures
3G, B-K Lighting, Ecosense, Lightcraft, Luminii,
RAB, Sistemalux, Tech Lighting, WAC Lighting
Mechanical
Mitsubishi, Panasonic, WhisperKOOL
Plumbing Fixtures
Kohler, Toto, Vigo, Watermark Designs
Wood Paneling
Vertical grain Douglas fir, mixed grain
White oak – Alamo Hardwoods

Awards

2024
SARA National Design Award, Excellence Award
SARA National Design Award, Additions and Small Projects Category

2023
Texas Society of Architects Design Award
Archello Awards, Winner Public Vote, Cafe/Restaurant of the Year

2022
AIA Small Projects Award
DNA Paris Design Award, Winner Residential Architecture
AZ Award of Merit
LOOP Design Awards, New Talent Award
LOOP Design Awards, Architecture Award

2021
Architizer A+ Award, Jury Winner, Bars & Wineries Category
Architecture MasterPrize, Best of the Best Small Architecture Category
Residential Architect Design Awards, Honor Award Outbuilding Category
Residential Design Architecture Awards, Honor Award
Gray Award, Winner, Residential Architecture Category
Luxe Red Awards National Winner, Wow-Factor Room
Luxe Red Awards Regional Winner, Wow-Factor Room
IFI Design Distinction Awards, Finalist
Frame Awards, Bar of the Year
The Plan Awards, Finalist

2020
AIA San Antonio People + Places Merit Award
Architect's Newspaper Best of Design Awards, Interior, Residential

Book Credits

Graphic Design by Florencia Damilano
Art Direction by Oscar Riera Ojeda
Copy Editing by Kit Maude

OSCAR RIERA OJEDA
PUBLISHERS

ISBN 978-1-964490-47-2
Published by Oscar Riera Ojeda Publishers Limited
Printed in China

Oscar Riera Ojeda Publishers Limited
Unit 1331, Beverley Commercial Centre,
87-105 Chatham Road South, Tsim Sha Tsui, Kowloon, Hong Kong

Production Offices
Suit 19, Shenyun Road,
Nanshan District, Shenzhen 518055, China

International Customer Service & Editorial Questions: +1-484-502-5400

www.oropublishers.com | www.oscarrieraojeda.com
oscar@oscarrieraojeda.com